MY WORLD OF SCIENCE

Magnetic and Nonmagnetic

Revised and Updated

Angela Royston

Heinemann Library
Chicago, Illinois

© 2003, 2008 Heinemann Library
a division of Capstone Global Library, LLC.
Chicago, Illinois

Customer Service 800-747-4992
Visit our website at www.capstonepub.com

Editorial: Rebecca Rissman
Design: Joanna Hinton-Malivoire
Picture research: Melissa Allison and Mica Brancic
Production: Duncan Gilbert

Originated by Chroma Graphics (Overseas) Pte. Ltd.
Printed in the United States of America in Eau Claire, Wisconsin.

072015
009073RP

ISBN 13: HB: 978-1-4329-1447-9, PB: 978-1-4329-1469-1

The Library of Congress has cataloged the first edition as follows:
Royston, Angela
Magnetic and nonmagnetic / Angela Royston
          p. cm. – (My world of science)
Includes bibliographical references and index.
Contents: What does a magnet do? – Magnetic materials- Are all metals magnetic? – Nonmagnetic materials – can magnetism pass through water? - Can magnetism pass through other materials? – Using magnets- Magnet in toys – Magnets and refrigerators – Magnetic rocks – The earth is a magnet – Using the earth's magnet – A compass.
ISBN 1-40340-855-6 (HC), 1-40343-168-X (Pbk)
1. Magnetism–Juvenile literature. 2. Magnets–Juvenile literature [1. Magnetism. 2. Magnets.] I. Title

QC753.7 .R69 2003
538-dc21   2002009434

Acknowledgements
The publishers would like to thank the following for permission to reproduce photographs: © Aviation Picture Library p. **29**; © Hardlines p. **25**; © Network Photographers p. **17**; © Trevor Clifford pp. **4, 5, 6, 7, 8, 9, 10, 11, 12, 13, 14, 15, 16, 21, 22, 26, 27, 28**; © Trip p. **23** (H. Rogers); unknown p. **24**; © Zul Mukhida pp. **18, 19, 20**.

Cover photograph reproduced with permission of Science Photo Library (Charles D. Winters).

The publishers would like to thank Jon Bliss for his assistance in the preparation of this book.

Every effort has been made to contact copyright holders of any material reproduced in this book. Any omissions will be rectified in subsequent printings if notice is given to the publishers.

Contents

Any words appearing in the text in bold, **like this**, are explained in the glossary.

What Does a Magnet Do?

A magnet has the power to pull some things towards it. Nails can be pulled onto a magnet. The magnet's pull holds them there.

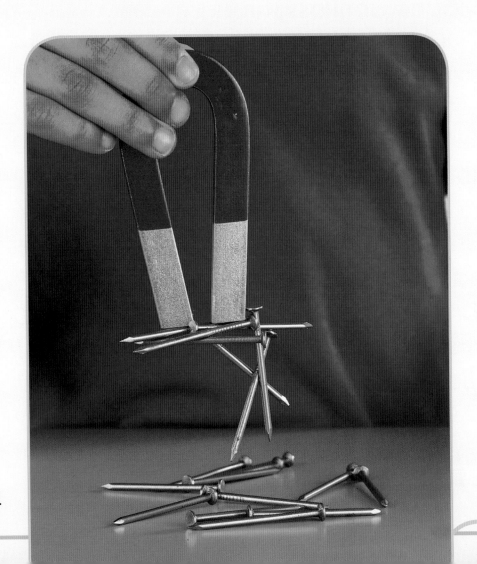

A magnet can pull things even when it is not touching them. The power of this magnet is lifting the nail into the air.

Magnetic Materials

Only some kinds of materials are pulled towards a magnet. You can use a magnet to test which kinds of materials are pulled towards it.

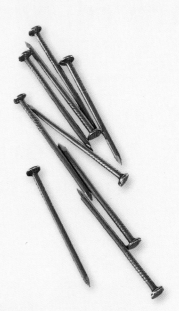

These things are all made of iron or steel.

A magnet can pull all iron and steel things towards it. Iron and steel are magnetic.

Are all Metals Magnetic?

The things in the picture are all made of metal. Only metal things can be magnetic, but not all metals are magnetic. Only iron and steel are magnetic.

silver

iron

aluminum

gold

copper

steel

Some cans are made of **aluminum**.
Others are made of steel. A magnet
does not stick to aluminum.

Nonmagnetic Materials

All the materials in the picture are nonmagnetic. When you touch them with a magnet, they do not stick to the magnet.

The silver-colored paper clips are made of steel. The rest are plastic. Plastic is nonmagnetic. What color are the magnetic paper clips? (Answer on page 31.)

Can Magnetism Pass Through Water?

This girl is testing to see if a magnet works in water. She has put a nail in a bowl of water and she is bringing the magnet close to it.

The nail has jumped onto the magnet
before the magnet has touched it. So
the pull of the magnet can pass through
the water to the nail.

Can Magnetism Pass Through Other Materials?

Cloth is nonmagnetic, but the pull of a magnet can pass through cloth to a magnetic object such as a nail.

These things are all too thick for the magnet to pull through them.

Magnetism only passes through thin materials. The pull of a small magnet is not strong enough to pass through thick materials.

15

Using Magnets

Many keys are made of steel, so they are magnetic. The key-holder in the picture is a long, thin magnet. The keys stick to it, so it is easy to find them.

This cat has a magnet on her **collar**. The magnet releases a catch on her cat flap when she pushes it from the outside. No other cat can get in.

17

Magnets in Toys

The **wagons** on this train are joined by magnets. The magnet on the front of one wagon sticks to the magnet on the back of the next wagon.

A travel game may use magnets to keep the pieces on the board. This means that you can play the game in a moving car or on a train.

Magnets and Refrigerators

Magnets stick to **refrigerators** because refrigerators are made of steel. You can use a magnet to stick a photograph to the door of a refrigerator.

rubber strip

A refrigerator door has a **rubber** strip around the edge. Below the rubber is a magnetic strip. The magnet sticks to the door to keep it tightly closed.

Magnetic Rocks

This rock is called fool's gold. It looks like **gold**, but it contains iron, not gold. Certain kinds of rock that contain iron are magnetic.

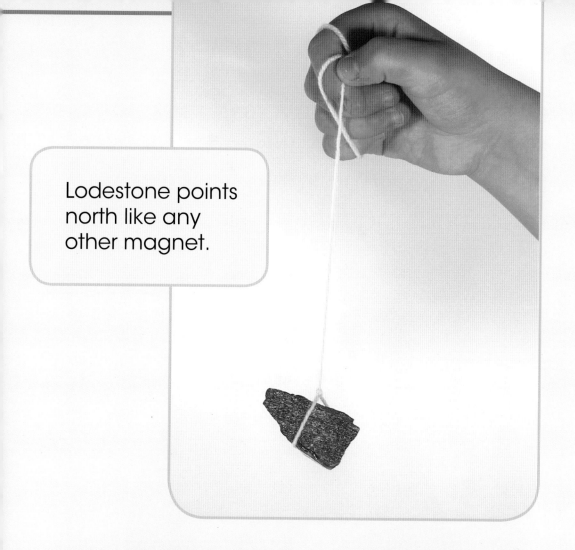

Lodestone points north like any other magnet.

Lodestone is a natural magnet. It attracts things made of iron and steel. Hundreds of years ago people used lodestone to make simple **compasses**.

The Earth Is a Magnet

The Earth consists of layers of rock. In the center is the core. It is made of very heavy iron. This iron core is like an enormous magnet.

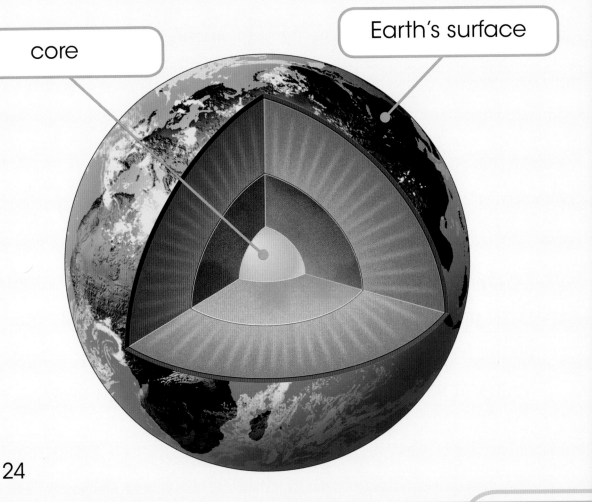

core

Earth's surface

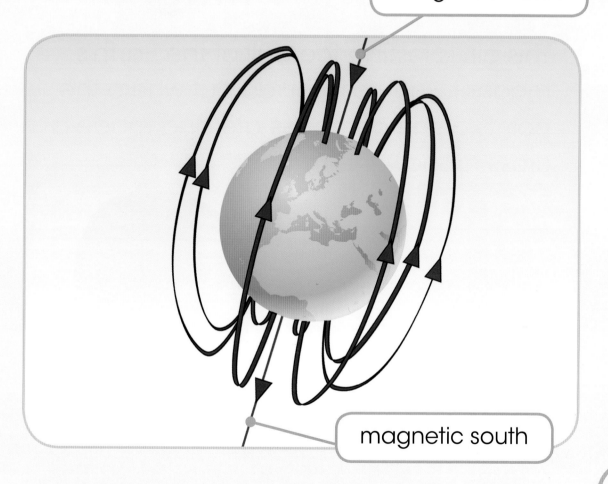

magnetic north

magnetic south

The Earth's magnet can be felt by other magnets. The red lines show how the Earth's magnet pulls other magnets towards the magnetic **north pole**.

Using the Earth's Magnet

This girl is testing the pull of the Earth's magnet. She has worked out where the points of the **compass** are and made a cross to show them.

This girl has tied a magnet to a string and let it swing over the points of compass.

points of compass

North

East

West

South

When the magnet stops swinging, one end points north. The same thing happens every time. Which way does the other end point? (Answer on page 31.)

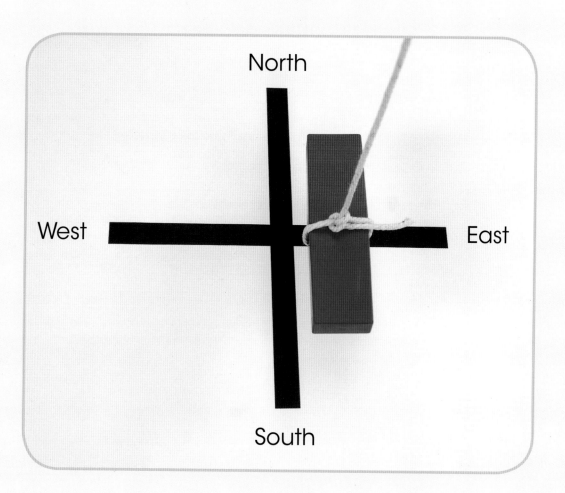

Compasses

A **compass** is an **instrument** used to find the direction of north. The needle is a small magnet. The rest of the compass is nonmagnetic.

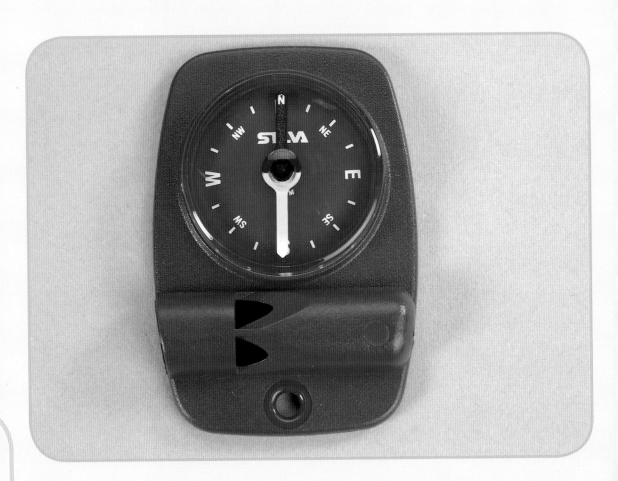

Ships and airplanes have a compass on them. The pilot of a plane checks the compass. He uses it to fly the plane in the right direction.

Glossary

aluminum a kind of metal that is nonmagnetic

collar something that is worn around the neck

compass instrument that shows the direction of north

gold a rare metal that is worth a lot of money

instrument tool

lodestone rock that forms a natural magnet

north pole the furthest north that you can go on Earth

refrigerator machine that keeps things cold

rubber a flexible material that is made from oil or the sap of the rubber tree

wagon big box on wheels that is used to carry things by rail

Answers

Page 11—The blue, red, green, and yellow paper clips are nonmagnetic. Only the silver-colored paper clips are magnetic.

Page 27—The other end of the magnet points south.

More Books to Read

Cooper, Christopher. *Magnetism: From Pole to Pole.* Chicago: Heinemann Library, 2004.

Royston, Angela. *Magnets.* Chicago: Heinemann Library, 2008.

Seuling, Barbara. *Earth Is Like a Giant Magnet.* Mankato, MN: Picture Window Books, 2007.

Index